Praise for *F*

*Freeing Yourself Financially* is an excellent guide for women seeking financial independence. This book takes you through all of the steps necessary to have a healthy management of your money and financial future with proactive tips for short and long term budgeting. It takes you through every step of understanding all the facets of budgeting, debt, saving and overall financial health. It shows you how to take control, gain and keep financial independence and it even connects the importance of financial and emotional health and re-building self-esteem.

----Malinda Everson, Development Director, DV & SA Advocate, Betty Griffin Center:


*Freeing Yourself Financially* is a must-have resource for survivors of abuse! This book gives practical advice on how to independently manage your finances. I work with several survivors who have stayed in their abusive relationship because the abuser maintains power and control over them through their finances. Most survivors are overwhelmed with even the thought of leaving because they're not sure how they're going to support themselves or their children. Kristin Paul delivers an accurate account on how to safely separate yourself from the grips of financial control. You will be empowered through the exercises and the self-care tools provided. *Freeing Yourself Financially* is an easy read and a useful guide to finding your voice again. I recommend this book for anyone who's ready to break free!

---Faith Joyner, LMFT, author of *Your Tool Guide for a Happy Marriage*

# Freeing Yourself Financially

*A Woman's Guide
To Rebuilding Her Finances
After Divorce*

by Kristin K. Paul

The content of this book is intended solely for informational purposes. The author strongly urges anyone who feels they need additional information or explanation to consult a financial adviser or accountant. The author has made every effort to ensure the accuracy of the information within this book was correct at the time of publication. The author and publisher assume no responsibility for any damages resulting from using the information or advice contained in this book.

COPYRIGHT © 2017 by Purple Ribbon Publishing
EDITOR: PT Editing
COVER DESIGN: Sprinkles on Top Studios

ISBN: 978-0-9963307-5-6

All rights reserved. No part of this work may be used or reproduced in any manner whatsoever without written permission of the author except in the case of brief quotations embodied in critical articles or reviews. For permission contact KristinPaul@yahoo.com or www.PurpleRibbonPublishing.com.

# TABLE OF CONTENTS

Introduction ............................................................................................. 1

## Part 1 Organize and Separate ................................................... 2

Chapter 1 Getting Organized ....................................................... 3
    Current:
    Privacy
    Documents
    Healthcare
    Valuables
    Household Information
    Future:
    Will
    Guardian
    Life Insurance
    Beneficiaries
    Divorce Decree
    Emotional Health

Chapter 2 Separating Financially ............................................... 7
    Assets
    Expenses
    Child and Spousal Support
    Organization
    Emotional Health

## Part 2 Income versus Expenses ............................................. 11

Chapter 3 Income ....................................................................... 12
    Identify Average Monthly Income
    Emotional Health

Chapter 4 Expenses ................................................................15
    Create Spreadsheet
    Log Expenses
    Create and Total the Categories
    Make Adjustment
    Emotional Health

Chapter 5 Current Financial Situation ........................................21
    Compare Expenses and Income
    Assets
    Liabilities
    Combine Statements
    Emotional Health

# Part 3 Creating a Budget—Improving Your Net Income ........25

Chapter 6 Increasing Income..................................................26
    Resume Current Job
    Switching Careers
    Part-time work
    Working from home
    Education
    Training
    Using Skillset
    Emotional Health

Chapter 7 Decreasing Expenses..............................................31
    Analyzing All Expenses
    Emotional Health

# Part 4 Look Deeper—Debt and Savings ..............................47

Chapter 8 Debt ..................................................................................48
    What Is Debt?
    Credit History
    Credit Report
    Credit Score
    Impact of Credit Score
    How can you strengthen your credit score
    No Credit Score
    Why Do We Have Debt?
    Tips
    Tackling Debt
    Emotional Health

Chapter 9 Savings and Goals ..............................................................57
    What Are Your Goals?
    Emergencies
    College
    Home
    Car
    Vacation
    Taxes and Extra Paychecks
    Retirement
    Different Types of Retirement Accounts
    Investing Your Money
    Long-term Planning
    Life Insurance
    Different types of life insurance
    Emotional Health

# Part 5 Putting It All Together ..............................................68

Chapter 10 Wrapping Up ....................................................................69
    Last Minute Information
    Emotional Health

Appendix A  Domestic Abuse ........................................................................ 71

Appendix B  Examples of Expenses .............................................................. 76

Acknowledgements ........................................................................................ 79

# Introduction

Welcome! *Freeing Yourself Financially* is the first step toward gaining control of your finances. If you have recently separated or divorced, you might feel overwhelmed when it comes to your personal finances. This is a common reaction. You've endured a difficult period and are now tasked with another stressor.

This step-by-step guide will help you navigate through several topics, such as creating a workable budget, reducing expenses, increasing income, dealing with credit card debt and life insurance matters, and saving for different goals. We will break every step down into smaller, manageable chunks. Each one of these steps will take time to accomplish, but the time you put into the exercises will be worth it. You will attain peace of mind and control over your finances, no matter what your current financial situation may be.

If your partner was in charge of the majority of your finances in the past, this area might be quite mysterious or alien to you. Confusion may reign and you may be bewildered as to the best place to start. *Freeing Yourself Financially* will help you work your way through the daunting task of creating a budget and sticking to it in order to gain financial independence and security.

Once you have completed the chapters in this book and have created a feasible budget, your anxiety over money and the future will decrease enormously. You will have a plan, something tangible to guide you through all movements as you progress forward.

Throughout *Freeing Yourself Financially*, we will take time to focus on your emotional health. Recognize that this is a very difficult time and transition for you. Realize that you can and might need to grieve. There have been many adjustments whether children are involved or not. You're learning how to become independent again, both financially and emotionally. You have suffered a loss and *Freeing Yourself Financially* honors that.

Strong emotional health leads to better decision-making. Emotional health affects your finances because how you feel influences your spending habits. Professional counseling for your mental health might be appropriate if you are struggling with the transition. If you have children, they could be suffering, too. All of you may benefit from counseling. This is an adjustment for you and your children. Find a counselor who is a good fit for your family. Be willing to try different counselors until you find the right one.

If you suffered domestic abuse, it is vital to seek help and healing to repair self esteem and deal with unresolved issues. Different types of abuse will be outlined in Appendix A.

*Freeing Yourself Financially* evolved from my own transition through divorce. I found myself confronted with tough decisions and sacrifices. I hope you benefit from my experiences.

# Part 1

*Organize and Separate*

# Chapter 1
## *Getting Organized*

In this first section we will focus on taking care of personal and family documents and valuables. Decisions will need to be made. Consider talking to family and close friends about some of the subjects in this chapter. You don't have to go through this process alone.

Let's work through a few vital issues that need to be taken care of as soon as possible.

• Privacy—One area of concern for some recently divorced women is the potential violation of their privacy. Make sure to change all passwords to bank accounts, email, children's school records, and credit cards. I suggest your new password be quite different from the previous one. Do you feel that your mail is vulnerable to inspection? Is a post office box necessary? This should be a consideration during a contentious divorce or in the instance of an abusive ex-partner. Information about abusive marriages is included in Appendix A.

• Documents—It is crucial to compile an inventory of important documents.

Do you have your Social Security Card? Your children's? If not, do you have the relevant Social Security numbers? This is essential information to possess for many reasons, including future registration of children in school, enrolling them in extracurricular activities, and claiming matters and items related to your children on your taxes. If you do not have this information, you can go to the Social Security office and apply for the cards. The numbers should be on your previous year's taxes. (Links to the Social Security Department website and many other websites are available at www.PurpleRibbonPublishing.com).

Gather copies of your birth certificate and your children's. If you do not have a physical copy, you can obtain copies by contacting the state where your child was born. (Go to PurpleRibbonPublishing.com for more information.)

If you own a home, do you have possession of the legal documents, such as the deed? If you can't find it, you can apply for a copy at your county courthouse. Do you have a copy of the mortgage loan information, including the real estate tax statement? If you rent, do you have a copy of the lease agreement? Your landlord should be able to provide you with a copy.

• Healthcare—Make sure you have your health and prescription insurance cards. Compile all details of your family's medical history. Keep doctors' phone numbers handy and write down a list of your family's prescriptions and dosages.

• Valuables—Any valuables, such as collectibles and jewelry, should be documented by taking photos of them. Keep the pictures in a safe place. You can either print them out or store them on an external computer device. If you are tech savvy, you could store them on a free cloud service such as Apple, Google Drive, etc.

• Household Information—Be sure to keep warranties for appliances, receipts for major purchases and owner's manuals in one location. These should be readily available in case you need them.

Let's go over planning for the future for a moment.

1) Last Will and Testament—Do you have a will? If you have children under the age of 18, have you designated their guardian in case you pass away? Is it their father? It is vital that you have a will which specifically designates a guardian for your children. Seeking advice from a lawyer is advisable.

2) Guardian Designation—This is a significant decision. Take your children's ages and the age of the potential guardian into account. Talk to the person(s) you are considering. How do they feel about raising your children? Ensure their understanding of the commitment.

3) Life Insurance—Once the legal guardian is decided upon and agreed to, you will need to purchase adequate life insurance to leave to the guardian to

cover the children's needs. If the guardian is their father, the terms of the divorce decree might require you to have a specific amount of life insurance and to designate him as the beneficiary.

If you have children over the age of 18, consider purchasing life insurance and listing them as the beneficiaries. Different types of life insurance will be reviewed in Chapter 9. (Go to PurpleRibbonPublishing.com for more information.)

4) Other Beneficiary Accounts—For retirement accounts, check who is listed as the beneficiary. Now that you are separated, do you want or need to change the nominated beneficiary?

**Divorce Decree**

If you are recently divorced, do you understand the financial terms that are outlined in the divorce decree? This knowledge is crucial to your financial well-being. If you are confused, please ask a lawyer or a legal representative to explain the details to you. If your ex-partner is not cooperating with the agreement, you may need assistance from a lawyer. You will be dividing assets and liabilities and want to make sure that the process goes smoothly and quickly. The faster the process is completed, the sooner you can start to create your budget and move forward with your life.

There were many topics covered in this section and working through them was very important. The task of organizing is sometimes difficult, but the steps you have taken are crucial to your financial well-being. Reading through all the suggested documents is not easy, but essential.

$ Have you taken care of privacy issues?
$ Did you gather important documents?
$ Healthcare information?
$ Inventory of valuables in a safe place?
$ Do you have relevant household information?
$ Do you have a will?
$ Did you designate a guardian?
$ Make sure to buy adequate life insurance
$ Do you need to change any beneficiaries?
$ Do you understand your divorce decree?

## Emotional Health

Understand that at this time you will require support from family and friends. Welcome their support. Talk to loved ones about your fears. Giving voice to concerns can ultimately help with the process of dealing with your situation and also help you solve problems. Keep a close network of friends, family, a counselor and church community to support you.

**EXERCISE:** Think about your relationships with others and your core group of supporters. List three people you can contact for support. They might fill different roles. A friend or sister might provide comfort when discussing the loss of your relationship. Someone in your church might comfort you spiritually. A trusted counselor could provide a foundation to rebuild lost self-esteem.

# Chapter 2
## *Separating Financially*

The process of separating financially from your ex-partner is essential to your financial well-being. Ensure your ex-partner possesses zero control over your financial affairs from this point on. In this section we will free you of the burden of being tied to him financially. This will significantly reduce future problems.

### ASSETS

It's time to gather records of all your financial accounts. All accounts jointly owned will need to be divided and closed. All bank accounts, retirement accounts and investment accounts should be separated according to the separation agreement or divorce decree. This step is not automatically completed. Contact each organization and provide the documents required. Following up on this step is essential.

One exception is a child's savings account. Both parents can be listed as the custodian. How are you planning on handling this account? Will you and your child's father be able to agree on how the money is spent on the child? If not, consider two separate custodian accounts, one with each parent listed as the custodian.

### EXPENSES

Compile a list of all your bills. Be sure to include those paid monthly, quarterly, semi-annually and annually, such as home and car insurance and annual maintenance fees. Your bank statements will indicate bills that are directly deducted from your account. If this compilation is difficult, start saving paper documents, such as statements and receipts, and an extensive list will naturally occur over a few weeks or months.

Take a look at each bill. Is the bill in your name only? Does it have you and your ex-partner's name listed? Should your name be taken off a bill? For example, did you move out of the house, but the electricity bill is still in your name? If it remains in your name and it isn't paid, your credit rating could be damaged. Ensure you are only paying bills that you are responsible for.

What loans are you responsible for? Do you have a car loan? Is that car yours or did your former partner get it, and is the loan in your name? What about a mortgage? Is your ex staying in the home? He will need to remove your name from the mortgage. You will need to make sure to follow up with these institutions. These bills will be shared/allocated according to the divorce decree.

What about credit cards? Does your former partner have access to any of your credit cards? If so, immediately cancel the card. You could be liable for any charges he makes. Has he opened a new card in your name and is he using it? This is a tactic used by financially abusive people. We will go through credit card issues in much greater detail in Chapter 8, and financial abuse in Appendix A. However, if you suspect your former partner is opening accounts in your name, skip to Chapter 8 and obtain your credit card report immediately.

This process is just like changing names on your assets. It can be time consuming and frustrating, but essential to address.

## CHILD AND SPOUSAL SUPPORT

Are you entitled to child support and/or spousal support (also known as spousal maintenance or alimony)? If so, are the payments directly deposited into your personal bank account? I highly recommend that this is set up as soon as possible. This will avoid disputes and prevent payments from being late. He will have no excuses about forgetting to give you a check if the money is being directly deposited.

## ORGANIZATION

Now that you have accumulated all of this information, and changed the names on the statements, it is time to create a filing system. You might choose to set up folders for each bill and keep them in a filing cabinet, or alternatively, organize this information on the computer in one file. Include the institution, the website for the account, account number, and customer service number to access the account information. Keep the passwords in a separate and safe place. If you have been paying bills automatically with either your joint bank account or joint credit card, make sure to contact the company and give them your new bank information.

You have accomplished a great deal by separating and splitting the accounts according to the divorce decree. Organizing your statements and bills will bring great peace of mind and avoid confusion and mistakes in the future. Have you completed this task? Yes? This was a huge process and commonly stressful, but you've completed it. Be proud. You are on your way to financial freedom.

$ Change all statements to your name only
$ Set up child support/spousal support as direct deposit
$ Organize all statements and bills

## Emotional Health

Don't forget about your body. Exercise! Activate those endorphins. Take walks, bike ride, hike, join a gym, or exercise. You could do this with your kids or grandkids. You can find videos for different exercises on YouTube or a cable channel. Ensuring great physical health is a precursor to great emotional health.

**EXERCISE:** List five fitness-related activities you've wanted to try. Dig deep into your mind. What activities have you always wanted to do, but have never taken the time to accomplish? Running, joining a gym, weight lifting, hiking, yoga, skiing, surfing or biking?

Put the ideas in order from least expensive (most reasonable for your current situation) to most expensive. Implement the first item on your list. This is a time for exploration. Good physical health will increase the mental focus necessary for financial decisions.

# Part 2

*Looking At Income And Expenses*

# Chapter 3
## *Income*

In Part 2 we will establish an intimate feel for your average monthly income and expenditure. As you work through these two chapters, keep in mind that the information will be used throughout the rest of the book.

Let's get started. We are going to identify your total monthly income. How is your pay distributed? Weekly, bi-weekly, monthly? Does your income vary? If commission forms part of your income, or hours worked differ week to week, we will identify a fair, yet conservative dollar amount to use as your monthly income total.

What does your total income include? Do you receive child or spousal support? Please note you must claim spousal support as income at tax time, so it is advisable to put aside a portion of what you receive. Do you have other sources of income such as part-time employment, dividend checks, rent from an investment property?

Often your pay includes many other benefits besides just the take-home pay. For example, do you have different forms of insurance benefits through your job? Health or life insurance? What about a retirement account? Medical flexible spending account (FSA)? (Go to www.PurpleRibbonPublishing.com for more information.)

### Scenario #1 chart

| EMPLOYEE NAME | AMOUNT |
|---|---|
| GROSS PAY | $1,600 |
| HEALTH INSURANCE | -$70 |
| FEDERAL WITHHOLDING | -$150 |
| SOCIAL SECURITY | -$100 |
| MEDICARE | -$30 |
| 401K CONTRIBUTION | -$50 |
| NET PAY | $1,200 |

## Income Scenario #1

In this example, the net pay bi-weekly is $1,200. So, on average the monthly take-home pay will be **$2,400**. Twice a year, she will receive an extra paycheck because bi-weekly occurs 26 times a year. We will discuss the extra two paychecks in Chapters 8 and 9.

This scenario shows that she pays $70 per pay period for health insurance. She is contributing $50 every pay period (26 times a year) to her retirement plan.

The second example calculates total monthly income by adding the weekly net pay (after taxes) for four weeks and monthly child support. This woman works different hours each week, so her income varies.

## Scenario #2 chart

| NET PAY | AMOUNT |
| --- | --- |
| 1ST WEEK NET PAY | $520 |
| 2ND WEEK NET PAY | $480 |
| 3RD WEEK NET PAY | $450 |
| 4TH WEEK NET PAY | $550 |
| MONTHLY CHILD SUPPORT | $400 |
| TOTAL MONTHLY TAKE-HOME PAY | $2,400 |

## Income Scenario #2

The total monthly net income for this woman is **$2,400**. Four times each year, she will receive an extra paycheck because she is paid weekly, or 52 times a year. We are calculating for four weeks per month and will discuss the extra four weeks in Chapters 8 and 9.

It is important and sometimes eye-opening to calculate how much income you are bringing in and then to see where it all goes. You are setting yourself up for financial freedom every step you take!

## Emotional Health

How do you feel about your current job? Are you content or would a career change be of benefit? Have you been a stay-at-home mom/wife and now need to enter the paid workforce? Is there a career you've always wanted to try? Could you build toward that?

**EXERCISE:** List 5 professions you've been interested in. Think back to your childhood. Allow yourself to dream. You might not be able to become an astronaut, but you could do something with astronomy. Make your list.

Now rearrange the ideas from most realistic to least realistic. Evaluate. This is a scary time to switch jobs, and now might not be the right time, but encourage yourself to widen your boundaries and identify possibilities. Is training available? Consider volunteer opportunities to broaden your outlook and to open new doors. An added benefit of volunteering is meeting likeminded people. And all volunteer work looks great on a resume.

So go ahead and let yourself dream. Good things will happen.

# Chapter 4
## *Expenses*

You've already accomplished so much! Now that we have looked at your income, let's look at your expenses. In this chapter we will identify your expenses and where you spend.

Let's be as specific as possible.

**Step 1**—Create a way to track spending

Create a system to log all spending. There are a couple of ways we can accomplish this, and no matter the method you choose be thorough and timely.

Try a spreadsheet on your computer. This method allows automatic totaling and grouping. There are online tools for creating a spreadsheet that you can download. There are even apps that you can use on your phone. (Go to www.PurpleRibbonPublishing.com for more information.)

You might prefer using a notebook and pen. When I first completed this exercise, I kept track of my spending in a notebook, and then at the end of the month transferred the data onto a spreadsheet on the computer. It worked for me.

**Step 2**—Log expenses

Keep a record of all of your spending for one month. Round up to the nearest dollar. If you spent $24.23 on gasoline, record $25. Did you buy a newspaper? A coffee? Lunch at work? Include everything, even the smallest items.

And now is not the time to change your spending habits. Do not pass judgement on what you spend your money on. Be honest and thorough. Log EVERY purchase. Our goal here is to draw an accurate picture of your current spending.

So, let's get started. The first column will be the date, the second is the item category, and third is the amount. Try to categorize your expenses specifically, so it will be easier to find out exactly how much money is going to certain areas. For example, if you shop at Walmart and spend $75 total on a gift, clothes, and groceries, break down the $75 and allocate appropriately to each.

Example for the beginning of January with a specific breakdown of Walmart expenses.

| 3-JAN. | GIFT | $20 |
|---|---|---|
| 3-JAN. | CLOTHES | $25 |
| 3-JAN. | GROCERIES | $30 |

This can be a daunting task and will be less stressful if you allocate a specific time each day to log your expenses. Keep all receipts and refer to bank and credit card statements to ensure no items are excluded. Remember to include expenses that may occur bi-monthly or yearly, insurances, school fees, childcare, gym memberships. Divide to be monthly appropriate. Look at prior spending in old checkbooks, bank accounts, credit card statements, all to jog your memory and identify things you may not have included. A comprehensive list of expenses and examples is located in Appendix B.

Let's look at this ALL EXPENSES FOR A MONTH SCENARIO...

|  |  |  |
|---|---|---|
| 1-JAN | RESTAURANT | $5 |
| 1-JAN | GROCERIES | $105 |
| 1-JAN | ELECTRIC BILL | $70 |
| 2-JAN | HOME MORTGAGE (INCL. TAXES & INSURANCE) | $700 |
| 2-JAN | RESTAURANT | $30 |
| 3-JAN | GIFT | $20 |
| 3-JAN | CLOTHES | $25 |
| 3-JAN | GROCERIES | $30 |
| 4-JAN | DAYCARE-FOR MONTH | $200 |
| 5-JAN | MEDICAL | $30 |
| 5-JAN | ENTERTAINMENT | $40 |
| 6-JAN | GROCERIES | $85 |
| 7-JAN | CAR LOAN | $200 |
| 8-JAN | HOME CLEANING | $10 |
| 8-JAN | PERSONAL CARE PRODUCTS | $15 |
| 9-JAN | CAR INSURANCE | $50 |
| 9-JAN | CABLE/INTERNET | $75 |
| 10-JAN | RESTAURANT | $25 |
| 10-JAN | GROCERIES | $75 |
| 12-JAN | ENTERTAINMENT | $20 |
| 12-JAN | GAS | $30 |
| 14-JAN | MEDICAL | $30 |
| 15-JAN | RESTAURANT | $5 |
| 15-JAN | ENTERTAINMENT | $25 |
| 17-JAN | TUTORING | $50 |
| 18-JAN | ENTERTAINMENT | $25 |
| 19-JAN | HOUSEHOLD ITEMS | $25 |
| 19-JAN | CLOTHES | $60 |
| 22-JAN | PERSONAL CARE PRODUCTS | $60 |
| 24-JAN | RESTAURANT | $5 |
| 25-JAN | GAS | $25 |
| 25-JAN | TRANSPORTATION | $40 |
| 27-JAN | CELL PHONE BILL | $75 |
| 30-JAN | ENTERTAINMENT | $25 |
| 30-JAN | GROCERIES | $110 |
| 31-JAN | MINIMUM MONTHLY CREDIT CARD PAYMENT | $100 |
| | TOTAL SPENDING FOR JANUARY | $2,500 |

Notice the total spending for January was $2,500. We want to get more specific and find out how much money was spent in each category. For example, how much money was spent on restaurants in January?

**Step 3**—Total the categories

| ITEM | AMOUNT |
| --- | --- |
| CABLE/INTERNET | $75 |
| CAR INSURANCE | $50 |
| CAR LOAN | $200 |
| CELL PHONE BILL | $75 |
| CLOTHES | $85 |
| DAYCARE FOR MONTH | $200 |
| ELECTRIC BILL | $70 |
| ENTERTAINMENT | $135 |
| GAS | $55 |
| GIFT | $20 |
| GROCERIES | $405 |
| HOME CLEANING | $10 |
| HOME MORTGAGE (INCL. TAXES & INSURANCE) | $700 |
| HOUSEHOLD ITEMS | $25 |
| MEDICAL | $60 |
| MINIMUM MONTHLY CREDIT CARD PAYMENT | $100 |
| PERSONAL CARE PRODUCTS | $75 |
| RESTAURANT | $70 |
| TRANSPORTATION | $40 |
| TUTORING | $50 |
|  |  |
| TOTAL FOR MONTH | $2,500 |
|  |  |

Now we can see what the spending was for each category. In this example, total spending on restaurants was $70. We will use this information in chapter 7 when we decrease expenses.

**Step 4**-Make Adjustment

One last step! You have the total amount of money that you spend each month. Add 'Adjustment' to your spreadsheet and to get this, multiply your total expenses by 5%. This will give you some cushion, in the event expenses increase.

| Total for month | $2,500 |
|---|---|
| 5% adjustment | $125 |
| Total for month with adjustment | $2,625 |

Great job! This section was very tedious and time-consuming, but you now have information that we will use in detail in Chapter 7.

## Emotional Health

Try not to be judgmental about your past and current spending. Don't justify expenses or cut any at this time. These are your bills and habits. Habits are hard to break, so go easy on yourself. You've been through a very difficult transition and your spending is what it is.

**EXERCISE**: Just notice how you are feeling when you are making incidental purchases. Are you happy? Depressed? Are you spending money based on your mood?

If you don't already do so, this could be a good time to start writing in a journal. Putting your thoughts and emotions down on paper can be a big step to emotional healing and can put your financial mindset into perspective.

# Chapter 5
## *Current Financial Situation*

Where do you stand now? Let's examine your financial situation as it is today. The only way to properly create a financial plan is to know your starting point.

Subtract your monthly total expenses from your monthly income. Is the result a positive figure? Are you spending more or less than you make? If a substantial amount of debt is your problem, you will discover steps to lessen the debt in Chapter 8. You might just need to tweak your spending or increase your income a little.

Let's look at the scenario we have been working with. This is the first step.

In each income scenario, the net pay for the month was $2,400. The total spending for the month was $2,625 (which includes an adjustment). So, we have a net loss of $225 per month. In the upcoming chapters we will discuss how to be able to have money left over by increasing income and decreasing expenses.

| Income | $2,400 |
|---|---|
| Expenses | $2,625 |
| Net income (loss) | ($225) |

The second step is to look at your assets (what you own) and your liabilities (what you owe). Let's pull out those account statements from your files and get to work. Our goal is to get a snapshot of your current net worth.

### ASSETS

Let's start with your assets which include possessions that can be converted to cash. You may have several different types.

Step 1: Liquid assets are cash, and funds held in checking and saving accounts, and money market accounts. What is the total amount held in all accounts?

Step 2: What assets do you possess that could be sold and converted to cash relatively easily? These are called current assets. Consider excess furniture items, toys or clothes the children have outgrown, collectibles, antiques, crafts you've made. In the process of selling these, consider eBay, Craigslist, Etsy for crafts, a garage sale, or a consignment shop.

Step 3: What about a Certificate of Deposit (CD)? If you have one, what is the amount invested, the interest rate, and the maturity date? The maturity date is the date you can withdraw your money without penalty. Will you pay a penalty for early withdrawal? Write this information down.

Step 4: Do you own investments (ex: mutual funds) that are not associated with a retirement account? What is the total of all of your investments? Write down the value of your investments.

Step 5: Do you own a car? What is the current value? Refer to 'Kelly Blue Book' and click on 'What's my car's value' if you require assistance. Apply a lower price to be conservative. (Go to www.PurpleRibbonPublishing.com for more information.)

Step 6: Any real estate? What is the value of any home or property you own? (Go to www.PurpleRibbonPublishing.com for more information.)

Step 7: Do you have a savings account for your child's college? Maybe a 529 savings account?

Step 8: How about a retirement plan? Does your employer deposit into one on your behalf? Is it called a 401K or 403b? If you aren't sure, ask your human resources manager. Do you have any kind of IRA? Maybe a Traditional or Roth? Do you have a claim to your ex-partner's retirement fund? Write down the sum value of these.

Step 9: Anything else of value not covered?

## LIABILITIES

Now let's address your liabilities and debt. List your loans. Include all credit card debt, personal loans, automobile loans, student loans, loans against your retirement account, payday loans, mortgage, home equity line of credit, and any other debt you may have.

Be specific when writing down the information. Be sure to include the payoff amount for each loan, not the monthly payment. This amount will be located on your monthly statement. You can also call customer service for assistance.

## COMBINE STATEMENTS

Let's look at the total value of your assets and liabilities and see where you stand. Calculate your total assets minus your total liabilities. This number gives you your net worth (loss) and we will use the information in later chapters.

$ Calculate your net income (income minus expenses)
$ List all your assets (what you own)
$ List all your liabilities (what you owe)
$ Calculate your net worth (assets minus liabilities)

## Emotional Health

What an accomplishment! You have compiled all of your financial information and rolled it into an understandable format, and now you have an accurate account of your financial situation.

How do you feel about the results of the statement? Relieved? Worried?

**EXERCISE:** Find 3 words to describe how you feel about your financial situation. Delve deeper into those words and expand on those feelings. Powerful emotions can come from this exercise. Remember to lean on a loved one during this time.

*Freeing Yourself Financially*

# Part 3

*Creating A Budget:
Improving Your Net Income*

# Chapter 6
## *Increasing Income*

We have completed a study of your assets and liabilities. Now we will brainstorm opportunities and ideas to earn more and spend less. Think about your skillset as you work through this chapter.

When considering an increase to your income, most people think of increasing work hours, whether it be returning to work, altering work type/place or obtaining additional employment.

### RESUME

Regardless of what avenue you wish to pursue to increase income, a résumé that shines is essential. There are many templates available online, or alternatively there are many companies which provide this service. Many local libraries offer informational sessions on résumé building.

Your résumé should include previous relevant work experience, education and training, and additional special skills you may have. Make sure to include volunteer work. Include a one-line summary of your job or career objective. Consider the type of references that will provide a positive picture of varied facets of your work ability, your work ethic, punctuality and loyalty, willingness to evolve and learn and try new things. Contact the people you chose to be sure they are willing to provide such references, and update them with your current skillsets and the reason you are seeking new work. Note that a reference sourced from volunteer work can add a layer of opportunity that other applicants may not have. Choose someone in a leadership role. Lastly, proofread your résumé. Eliminate typos and bad grammar, and double check that all relevant facts pertaining to the work you are applying for are included.

### CURRENT JOB

Do you currently have a job? Consider avenues to increase your income in this position. Are you due for a pay raise? Are more hours available? Is there an opportunity to take on new responsibilities in exchange for an increased pay rate? Perhaps work on a special project? If no progression is possible, consider searching for a position with a company that pays more and still has equivalent or better benefits.

## ANOTHER CAREER

What about pursuing another type of career? Maybe this idea makes you anxious. Do you have transferrable skills and experience that can be used in another area? Pull from all of your skillsets. For example, teachers have organization and communication skills which could be transferred into a real estate career. Volunteer work shapes varying skillsets. Did you organize a successful fundraiser? You now have skills that may be sought after in a development team that deals with fundraising. Think broadly. A travel agent could become a secretary or a tour guide. A nurse could use her experience and communication skills to become a corporate consultant. Receptionists make great information clerks, customer service representatives, and administrative assistants. After working in the retail field, people can transfer their skills into any job in sales, including insurance sales. A social worker can take her skills and work in human resources. If you are bilingual, you can find a job that needs your language skill.

## PART-TIME WORK

Would this offer an opportunity to supplement your income? Is this feasible when considering the logistics of your family life?

## WORKING FROM HOME

For decades this has been a growing enterprise. Could you work from home and generate income? There are many different types of jobs that allow you to venture into this style of work. You could become a virtual assistant, especially if you have computer skills. Is starting you own business possible? A consulting business? Or how about direct sales, such as Mary Kay or Avon? Nurses can work on-call evenings. Switchboard operators for medical clinics can work from home during their afterhours services. What about learning the skill of a medical coder? There are many opportunities for support and service jobs from home, such as: a customer service representative, an insurance support representative, or product support specialist. Travel agents and reservations agents can work from home. If you have computer graphic skills, you could create websites or graphics on the side. If you excel in accounting, you could be a bookkeeper or do taxes from home. You could work in sales and cold call.

## EDUCATION

Consider classes at a college or trade school near you. You may be eligible for free tuition. Contact the Financial Aid Office at the school. Research grants and ask about scholarships. Financial assistance is available.

Time away from home may not be viable. Consider online classes. These generally are set up so you are not required to check in at a specific time. You could work on the class in the evening, possibly after your children have gone to bed and/or early in the morning. This is a sacrifice, but is also an investment. Education is beneficial. It is an investment in you. Every experience you attain adds to your skillset.

Is full-time study an option? Consider a new field. The social aspect of attending classes will offer networking capabilities. You could try a new and unfamiliar subject. Some can be overwhelmed at the thought of attending college as a non-traditional student. Consider one class and see how it goes.

## TRAINING PROGRAM

Take a workshop or participate in a training program. Your employer may offer these, especially when you are required to remain current in particular skillsets or a changing work environment. Any workshop or training opportunity will add to your experience and make you more marketable. Take advantage of these.

## YOUR SKILLSET

Think about your hobbies or interests. Could they generate any additional income?

If you possess craft and artistic talents, consider creating items and selling them. There are several different outlets for selling crafts, including Etsy, craft fairs, eBay, specialty shops, home parties.

Do you have a degree in one of the various English college subjects? Editing, proofreading college papers, and helping with résumés are just a few examples of how to turn this asset into income.

If you are home during the day, consider a dog-walking business. It offers exercise which helps stimulate the brain.

*Freeing Yourself Financially*

How about babysitting? If you have kids, offer a service where the children come to your home.

Do you like to restore furniture?

Do you have teaching experience? Good tutors are in high demand and the pay is good. Could you teach a class at your local college?

If you are a talented photographer, consider a small business taking family portraits, or take landscape photos to sell.

Are you a stay-at-home mom/wife and feel the strain of not having 'workplace' experience? Examine your roles and list the skills you possess. All would look great on a résumé: communication, time management, budgeting, and logistics.

Once you have implemented ways to increase your income, your financial situation will improve.

## Emotional Health

Stepping out of your safety zone and trying something new can be challenging for many people. This is a great time for you to open yourself up to new possibilities. You're starting another chapter in your life, so enjoy the growth and take every opportunity that comes your way.

There are so many different jobs available. We really can't grasp all of the opportunities available to us.

**EXERCISE:** Locate job or career websites. Click to search for jobs. Find a job title you have never heard of that piques your interest. Read the job description. Find others that sound interesting. This illustrates the plethora of roles out there.

# Chapter 7
## *Decreasing Expenses*

In Chapter 4 we calculated your monthly expenses. We included most or all of your bills and spending. Have you purchased anything lately that wasn't included on your spending statement? If so, adjust your statement accordingly.

When we create a budget, we don't want it to be too rigid nor too frugal. Achievable steps with discipline will have a large impact.

We will now look at a wide variety of expenses that people generally work through. You will have several of the expenses that were listed in Appendix B, and maybe a few that are not included. You can add and delete expenses into your spreadsheet as needed. Be as creative as possible when coming up with ways to save money.

This is a good time to include children. Not only will they learn a valuable lesson, but they will also understand why you are making changes to your spending habits.

Let's look at every expense on your spreadsheet and identify ideas on how to cut some bills. Remember, life is give and take. If you spend money on one thing, you will need to give up something else.

Many of the expenses listed below will not apply to you. Concentrate on the expenses you have and want to cut back on.

All are broken down into categories. This chapter holds a lot of information and advice. You might find it easier to work on one section and then take a break before moving on to the next. Take a step by step approach.

### HOUSING

Think about your current housing situation. Do you own or rent? Have you considered downsizing into a less expensive home or apartment?

There are benefits to downsizing. Your taxes, utilities and home owners insurance will decrease. The equity in your home can be utilized to refinance and lower your mortgage payment, pay off some debt, or can be deposited into a particular savings account as discussed in other chapters.

If you downsize and purchase a townhome or condo, find out how much the Homeowners Association (HOA) fees are and what they cover. They should cover landscaping, snow removal, garbage pickup, possibly some utilities, and any amenities the complex has to offer, such as a pool or exercise room. Although the fees may seem high, compare the amount to your previous spending on those expenses.

Look at your current homeowner's insurance policy. You might have a low deductible. If you increase your deductible, your insurance premium will decrease, reducing your bill. Call your agent and ask for some quotes. Shop around for all of your insurance needs. Grouping all your insurance needs (home, car, life) with the same company may provide an overall discount.

What about refinancing the home you currently own? What interest rate are you currently paying on your mortgage? A 1.5% savings will decrease your mortgage payment greatly.

Are you renting? Does the place suit your current needs? Could you move closer to the city and use public transportation or move further out into a less expensive area? Always keep safety in mind.

## UTILITIES

Electricity/gas usage can be decreased with a few minor adjustments. Program your thermostat. Set the thermostat to suit your needs while your household is active, then conserve at night and when away.
Purchase energy efficient systems. When you change your light bulbs, replace them with energy efficient bulbs.

Take other simple steps, such as lowering the water heater temperature especially when on vacation, caulking windows, and making sure to turn off fans and lights before you go to bed.

Water bills. You can lower your water bill with a few quick adjustments. Run the washing machine and the dishwasher only when full, install water efficient toilets, take shorter showers, don't hand wash dishes, and fix dripping faucets.

Cable/phone/internet. There are several things you can do to cut these expenses, depending on how much you need each service. If you want all three, shop around. When purchasing multiple services together, the cost typically decreases. Negotiate with the cable company. Ask for promotions and sales.

If you are willing to drop or cut back on the services, you have many options. Many people have cell phones and don't even use their home phones. Drop the home phone. Now you are dealing with just cable and internet.

For the cable, think about what channels or types of shows you absolutely have to have. If you are a news junkie, you can go online, read and watch the news articles and clips. The internet offers so much more news access.

What about movies and TV shows? Have you thought about scaling back the TV channels you already have? You probably don't watch most of the channels you have access to. Can you talk to the cable company and subscribe to fewer channels?

There are several other great ways to access movies and TV shows. Netflix, Hulu, Roku, Amazon Prime, Apple TV, and gaming devices give you access to many for a minimal cost. Libraries have many DVDs for loan.

Cell phone. Cell phone bills can be very expensive, especially if you have children who are on your plan. There are several things you can do to cut the expense. First, look at past bills and determine your family's usage. How many minutes did you use on average for the last few months? Texts? Data? By analyzing your bill, you can identify a plan that will work best for your family. Are you willing to sacrifice and make changes, such as drop the data portion? If so, this will save you a lot of money. Does it make sense to have a maximum number of minutes or texts allowed?

Talk to your current cell phone company. Determine your needs, not wants. Then shop around. Better deals may be offered at electronics stores or warehouse stores. Several times each year companies have promotions offering great savings. Discuss discounts available when combining cable, internet and cell phone.

Do you receive a discount on your cell phone bill based on your place of employment? Tell the provider where you work and ask if a discount applies. If you have a data plan with limited usage, make sure to use WiFi as much as possible to avoid exceeding your data maximum.

## HOME MAINTENANCE AND CARE

Learn how to complete minor home repairs, such as changing your heating system filter and your water filter in your refrigerator. Discover the use and varied applications of a drill. Costs of labor can be astronomical, and with many tasks being simple, costs are often unnecessary. Tips are available on YouTube, or check out DIY books at your library.

A tool box should include a drill, screw driver set, WD40, super glue, hammer, tape measure, razor, knife and paint supplies.

Landscaping/Snow Removal: Are you using a service right now? Shop around for a less expensive service. Consider sourcing help from neighbors. Having a low maintenance lawn would be easier to maintain yourself.

Home Cleaning Supplies: Before spending a lot of money on cleaning products, consider using natural products such as vinegar, lemon juice and baking soda. Also use all-purpose cleaners whenever possible and purchase while on sale and with a coupon. Dollar stores have great deals on cleaning supplies. A tip: glass cleaner will clean almost anything and is sold at dollar stores.

Household Items/Furniture: Search garage sales, thrift and consignment shops and liquidation sales for these items. If you need furniture, ask friends and family if they know of anyone who is getting rid of theirs. Craigslist is also a good place to look. If you find store furniture that you're interested in, try negotiating a deal. Some stores are willing to drop their price to make a sale.

## TRANSPORTATION

What are you currently using for transportation? A car? Public transportation? First consider your automobile. Now that you are separated, does the car you own suit your needs? Think about what you use it for. Do you travel a long distance to work? Are you driving children to activities?

You might have a larger car and no longer desire or need that size. Could you trade it in for something smaller? Smaller cars generally get better gas mileage. Is the smaller car less expensive? If so, the monthly payments would be lower.

You want a car that is reflective of budget and your lifestyle. Maybe you were allocated the smaller car in the divorce, but you have three growing kids. In this case, you might need to save to purchase a larger car within the next couple of years.

Where do you park at work? Is there a parking fee? Do you have to pay to park in a parking garage? Is there a parking option that might be further away from your place of employment but cheaper? Is carpooling an option? This will cut down on your auto expenses, including gasoline. Look at all options available to you.

Ensure regular maintenance. Diligent maintenance and oil changes as per the recommended number of miles will pay for itself by requiring fewer repairs.

Again, shop around for car insurance. It is a very competitive market. Look into increasing your deductible, especially if you don't have a history of insurance claims. Increasing your deductible will reduce your premiums.

## GROCERIES

Grocery shopping can consume a large portion of your budget. There are several strategies you can use to decrease your grocery bill.

Preparation is key. It is imperative that you have a detailed grocery list and you stick to it. No extras. Study store flyers and plan meals based on the store sales. Develop ideas for a weekly meal schedule, including snacks, using the items on sale. Try to shop, at most, weekly because the less often you are in the store, the fewer impulse items you will purchase. This also saves on gas and time.

Coupons can be found in the Sunday paper and often online. Your grocery store might have coupons that you can upload to a phone app. And remember, the fewer distractions you have at the store, for example small children, the more success you will have.

Many stores run 'buy one, get one free' sales. These opportunities are a great way to stock up on items. However, only purchase them if they are an item you normally use. Also, watch the expiration date.

Large box stores are a good way to save money. Generally when items are purchased in bulk, the unit price is lower. Sometimes the sale at the grocery store can be cheaper, so get an idea for prices over time.

Store brand items are normally cheaper than name brand items, except when an item is on sale. If you are buying a product that isn't on sale, check to see if the store brand item is cheaper and don't forget the dollar stores. You can pick up good deals there, such as inexpensive storage containers, greeting cards and school supplies.

Alcohol is expensive. Could you cut back on your consumption? This could add up to a considerable savings.

Meat is generally expensive. Stock up on sales and when you purchase the meat in bulk, freeze it in meal size portions. Consider eating meatfree once or twice each week. When making casseroles with meat, cut the amount of meat added in half. Focus on the carbs and vegetables. You may be lucky enough to have no one notice the change. Buy cheaper cuts, such as round, flank, ground beef, brisket or chuck. Keep leftovers in the freezer for a stew. Shop at different stores, such as warehouse stores, Aldi, or an international store for less expensive prices.

A revolving monthly meal schedule can bring great success to your budgeting. It takes some planning the first time you do it, but then it's done and can be used for future months. This way you know exactly what your weekly list will be and you can look ahead and take advantage of sale items.

Keep nutrition in mind. Is a vegetable garden an option? Even a small garden can save money, and of course, the benefits of eating fresh and healthy are invaluable. Frozen fruits and vegetables are also a healthy choice and can be purchased in large quantities when on sale.

A great way to save money and time is to cook a large quantity of a recipe, then divide it into a few meals, and freeze for a later date. If you can utilize the sales and bulk purchases, this really cuts your grocery bill down.
Take leftovers to work for lunch. Purchasing lunch every day can be very expensive. If you spend $6 every day on lunch each week, that is $30 per week, or about $1,500 per year!

## RESTAURANTS

Previous exercises have identified your total expense in this area. Were you surprised by the amount spent? Could your money be redirected to more necessary items? Think about if your yearly expense in this area equates to $2,000, imagine the benefits of using that sum of money to pay off credit card debt.

Alternatively, consider reducing the number of times you eat out, making the experience a special occasion. Research restaurants that offer coupons and early bird specials. The prices of drinks add to the bill. A soda can cost $3. If four people order soda, that's $12, plus tax and tip. Consider ordering water instead. This would create a savings of $600 per year for a family that dines out weekly. Choosing to dine out for lunch instead of dinner often equates to a smaller bill. And don't forget to take home what you have not eaten.

## CLOTHING

Create an inventory of what you own. Go through all your clothes. What fits? What don't you like? What is in poor condition? Group into those you will keep and those you will donate or consign. When donating to a non-profit organization consider tax options; itemize for tax deductions. If you consign clothes, you will either receive money back or store credit.

Before purchasing new clothes, evaluate your needs. Shop for specific items that go with multiple clothes, such as a simple black skirt or tan pants.

Go to the store that sells the exact article of clothing you are looking for. Try not to browse.

Shopping for children is essentially the same as for you. If you have more than one child, hand-me-downs are great. Keep used clothes in a box labelled with the size. Consider consignment stores and thrift shops for children's clothes as the kids aren't in them for long.

Shop at sales and clearance outlets and never pay full price. It can be tempting when you receive email coupons from various stores to go out and shop. Be disciplined. Store these emails in a folder and when the need for shopping appears, check if any of the coupons match what you need at the store.

Always ask yourself if the item fits your specific need and what it might cost on sale in a different store. Discount chains and warehouse stores often have inexpensive clothing. For your basic clothing needs, such as workout clothes and t-shirts, shop generic.

You might have a friend who is the same size and wears the same style of clothing as you. Swap outfits once in a while. You will be wearing something that feels new to you, and at the same time expanding your wardrobe for free. Accept hand-me-downs from friends.

Do not buy 'dry clean only' clothes unless you can dry clean them at home. Dry cleaning expenses increase the cost of the item. Alternatively, dry cleaning sheets can be purchased to minimize the number of times you take items to the cleaners.

Learn to sew and mend basic things, such as a small rip or tear, or replace a button. For worn out knees in jeans or sweats, turn them into shorts.

Purchase out of season clothes. Clearance prices can be generous and will build your wardrobe more inexpensively. This works well for coats, too. Be cautious when shopping out of season for your children to ensure the item will fit when the season arrives. Buy only what fits!

Other Accessories: Ideally, you only need two purses: one for summer and one for winter. If you buy neutral colors you can use them all season. You never have to worry about clashing with your outfit or forgetting to transfer an item, like your wallet, when switching purses. Get a good quality purse that is large enough to use all the time.

Make sure you have a good pair of sneakers and neutral colored shoes. If you apply the strategy of wearing basic colors, such as black, tan, navy and white, then you will need fewer shoes. Buy good quality shoes and take care of them.

To add color, consider your accessories. Scarves and jewelry can add color to any outfit, but be thrifty, not indulgent.

## PERSONAL CARE

Let's start with shampoo and conditioner. There are several ways to save money when choosing your hair cleaning products. If you can't part with the more expensive products, at least try to purchase them while on sale and with a coupon. Buy the product that has the lowest unit price. Generally it will be the largest size, but check to be sure. Generic products will normally be the cheapest options, unless you get a great deal using coupons and sales. Stock up when the price is at its lowest. Haircare products at hair salons are very expensive. Avoid, or use sample products. When applying shampoo or conditioner, look at how much you are using. Can you use a little less?

Purchasing other toiletries, such as toilet paper, are generally cheapest when buying in bulk at a warehouse store.

Think about products such as makeup remover, cotton swabs, cotton balls and hair accessories. A great place to purchase these items is a dollar store.

For skin care and makeup, buying online can be less expensive. Try generic skin care products and lower priced makeup. Are you happy with the value? If not, watch for sales for your favorite brands. I always use a daily moisturizer that has sunscreen included in it. This skips a sunscreen step. Try buying your makeup and skin care products at a drug store. They are often cheaper, offer good sales, and will allow you to return the item if you find that you don't like the color. Add a few drops of saline to make dried out mascara usable. You can reuse good quality mascara brushes by rinsing them off with hot water. Paint brushes are also great tools to apply eye shadow. You can fix broken lipstick by heating it with a hairdryer. When you apply moisturizer and body lotion, apply after showering to damp skin. Try trial sizes first and ask for samples.

Who doesn't love a pedicure and a manicure? I'd love to indulge more frequently, but these can be very pricey. By stretching out the 'time between' you can create an impressive yearly savings. You can shop around to find the least expensive place to have your nails done. Could you just go without? Can you give yourself a manicure? How about getting together with a friend and doing each other's nails?

You can also save money on haircuts. If you get your hair cut every four weeks, stretch it out an additional week. You would save the price of two and a half haircuts per year, and in many cases this represents a savings of $100 or more. Consider a simple haircut. Shop around for a cheaper salon. If you have boys, can you cut their hair? Can you trim your hair or your daughter's bangs?

Is there a local beauty school where you could get your hair cut and colored for free or a reduced rate? Long hair generally requires less care and cutting. Maintain healthy hair by shampooing less frequently and doing a weekly conditioning treatment, and by taking multi-vitamins and Vitamin C to ensure your hair is getting the appropriate nutrients.

Only use one hair color and touch up your roots yourself. This will save a lot of money. After coloring your hair, don't wash for at least two days and protect your hair from the sun and chlorine.

## MEDICAL

It is crucial to practice preventative healthcare. Try not to miss your annual doctor's appointment, including blood work, mammograms, eye appointments, dental exams, etc. Detecting issues early is essential to good health, and can also prevent excessive expenditure later.

Prescription medication is cheaper when generic brands are purchaed. Consider mail order prescription companies and request a three month supply instead of one month. This can often cut costs. Some pharmacies offer certain medications for free. Check with your pharmacy and also shop around. Your employer might offer the opportunity to enroll in a Medical Flexible Spending Account. (Medical FSA) This is a pre-tax account that you use to pay your medical expenses. Talk to your human resources department about this. It can potentially save you hundreds of dollars each year in tax savings. (More information is available at www.PurpleRibbonPublishing.com.)

Keep all medical receipts, including copays and prescription receipts for your taxes. You might be able to claim some of the money spent on medical needs depending on your income level.

## CHILDREN AND CHILDCARE

As children age, their expenses increase. Sports, music/art lessons, tutoring, etc. can add up quickly.

Does your child need to be on a travel sports team? Do you have the time and money for the commitment that comes with it? Could they join the school team for free instead?

We want to give our children the world, but at times it's just not feasible. Maybe they want to learn horseback riding and karate. Consider allowing one activity, and explaining the reasons. Not only will they understand why they need to choose, but such an introduction into the world of decision making will equip them for the future.

Consider suggesting to your family to gift necessary items for birthdays etc. Bats and balls and footwear, summer sports camp, and musical instruments, karate uniforms.

Childcare: Childcare, daycare, pre-K and after school care can chew away a good portion of your budget. You want a high quality facility for as low cost as possible. How can you make this happen? Other parents can be your greatest resource for information.

Some childcare centers have sliding scale fees based on your income, and many offer a discount if you have more than one child enrolled. Check if your employer offers a Dependent Care Flexible Spending Account (Dependent care FSA). This is when you use pre-tax dollars to pay for qualified childcare expenses. Inquire with your human resources department. It could save you hundreds of dollars. (More information is available at PurpleRibbonPublishing.com.)

Be forewarned. Late pick up of children from childcare can cost you. Some centers charge as much as $5 per minute after a specific grace period. Make backup plans are in place in the event you are running behind. Perhaps offer a reciprocating agreement to another parent.

A sick child can often mean missed work. Do you have a family member who can help you out in these circumstances? A babysitter? Sometimes employers do not understand when you are forced to take time off due to a child's illness. Although unfair, it could reflect poorly or translate negatively on your job performance.

Another way to cut down on childcare expenses is to swap babysitting with another parent. This could also be done with afterschool care. A babysitting co-op with other mothers could benefit everyone.

Is it possible to work from home or can you work flexime? Flextime allows you to split your work time between your place of employment and home. This can be especially helpful if you have school-age children. It also cuts down on gas expenses and time. The saved money can be spent on necessities.

## GIFTS

If you have a large family, holidays and birthdays can become expensive. Consider a secret Santa within specific family/friendship groups. Can you make handmade gifts for family and friends? Necessities, such as coats and shoes, can now become good presents.

For children, set a budget and stick to it. It is more important for your family that you are financially free in the long run. When you spend more than planned, you will be more stressed, and everyone feels the tension. A happy home is most important.

Make a budget for gifts. For example, you could set aside $25 per month for gifts throughout the year. Alternatively, and more productive, consider cutting out all gifts until you are financially stable.

## EDUCATION

If you want to assist your child with college expenses, consider using a 529 plan. This is discussed further in Chapter 9. State colleges are less expensive than private universities. Community colleges are even less expensive than a four year state university. Your child could live at home and go to a community college to earn an associate's degree and then transfer to a four year university.

There are many scholarships and grants available. Be sure to talk to the financial aid counselor at the school.

Your child has opportunities to work at the school as well. They can apply to be a resident assistant and receive free or reduced dormitory fees. They could work on campus or near the school to cover their spending money and books. They will have access to student loans as well.

If you are returning to school, check with the financial aid office. You may be eligible for free or reduced tuition.

## FAMILY FUN

Entertainment: There are many, many ways to cut entertainment expenses. Going to the movies can be a great expense. Consider a DVD night at home with homemade popcorn etc.

Are you a member of a gym? Consider canceling your membership and finding alternative exercise, such as running or biking or walking through your neighborhood. Could you lift weights in your home? Participate in aerobics sessions using a DVD or YouTube?

Discover museums, art centers, historical sites that allow free entry. Go on picnics. Take advantage of these opportunities. Many theme parks and zoos offer annual passes.

Subscriptions to newspapers and magazines can add up. Are these essentials or entertainment? Can you access essential information online?

Book readers love purchasing books. Consider eBooks due to their comparably lower cost. You can also borrow magazines, DVDs and CDs from the library.

Vacation: Think of places to visit that suit your budget. If you want to go on a more extravagant vacation, save for it. This might mean you skip a year or two of vacation in order to go on a nicer one the following year. Do not steal from the budget.

## PETS

Owning a pet brings with it large expenses and is a hefty time commitment. Consider carefully before adopting or purchasing. Make sure to take your pet to the veterinarian for their annual checkup and ensure they stay current on their shots.

It can be very expensive if you need to board your pet when you go on vacation. Try to find someone who pet sits to save money. How about swapping pet sitting duties with another family who has pets?

## DONATIONS

Churches and charities need more than money to sustain themselves. They need your time. Your time is a gift in itself. Many charitable groups are looking for volunteers to help in all sorts of ways. Have you received assistance from a charity that you'd like to give back to? Did you support a charity financially in the past but you can't afford to now? Why not volunteer? Volunteering doesn't benefit the organization only. You will create a network of people which could serve you well in the future.

## LAWYER

Some separations require the use of lawyers for periods longer than others. Consider mediation. This is often a much less expensive and less stressful place to negotiate. If you were in an abusive marriage, then I would not suggest mediation. You don't want to be in a situation where the abuse can continue.

There are several advantages to mediation if both sides are willing. Mediation allows both parties to come to a decision instead of relying on a court to decide. You are still represented by a lawyer. Mediation can take much less time than going to court and therefore, a lot less money. You have more control in the decision making process.

## CONCLUSION

We all have a fixed amount of money and need to make choices when spending. Our decisions impact us not only today, but also in the future. When making decisions, don't only look at the price tag, but also consider the quality of the item. Quality items will last longer.

Remember, each time you spend money that wasn't budgeted for, you're taking money away from something else that was budgeted for. Morning coffee, buying lunch at work, buying a splurge item that you don't really need will impact your budget substantially.

Keep working to decrease your expenses. Get creative and remember what is most important to you.

You've reduced expenses and now the gap between your expenses and income has changed. What is your current net income? If it is still a loss after completing these chapters, consider seeking government assistance, and research your eligibility for assistance with housing, food stamps, health insurance, tuition and other essentials.

## Emotional Health

Many emotions can be triggered when we discuss spending money. Many times people spend money on wants because they feel they deserve the item. This could be a car, a massage, going out to a nice restaurant, anything that does not fit in with the budget.

We all want nice things. The key to this book is to teach yourself how to budget for them and not borrow beyond your means. We have to admit that sometimes we cannot afford everything we want. We need to remember to save for our future as well.

**EXERCISE**: Identify 3 things that you would like to have, but cannot afford. List these items in order from greatest want to least.

Look at the first item on your list. Can you save for it? Can you save to buy a cheaper version? Suppose it is a new car. Could you wait a year and save and then see if a used model fits in your budget?

Being thrifty doesn't mean you will never have what you want. It just means there will be some give and take. Sometimes compromises will be made.

# Part 4

*Look Deeper:
Debt And Savings*

# Chapter 8
## *Debt*

In Chapter 5, we looked at where you stand in terms of debt. Where did it come from? Marital debt? Spending more than you earned? A job loss? Student loans? Do you have a lot of high interest loans? This information impacts your financial plan. As you worked through your current financial situation, you gathered the specific information and data. Now we will delve deeper into the meaning of debt and look at ideas for reducing it. If you do not have debt, or have little, but also the ability to pay it off relatively easily and in a timely fashion, you may still find valuable information in this chapter. For those wrestling with debt, remember to call on emotional support from close friends if you become overwhelmed.

### What is debt?
Any time you borrow money/take out a loan you are using a line of credit. This debt is considered a liability.

### Credit history:
What is your record of paying back debt? Always on time? Late? In default? This affects your ability to obtain further credit, or a loan.

### Credit report:
It is imperative that you obtain your credit report. As mentioned earlier, this report will identify debt in your name, even debt that you do not know about. Many have discovered debt applied for by an ex-partner. If this situation arises, address it immediately by contacting the credit bureau.

A credit report also shows how you have dealt with debt in the past, if you are paying bills on time now, and what the monthly payment is. It shows the credit limit on each credit card, revolving debt you have, and loan balances. The credit limit is important to creditors because it shows how much access to borrowing you have. You might only have two credit cards, but if each credit card limit is $15,000, the total amount of money you have access to is $30,000. This could scare off potential lenders.

There are three reporting agencies that keep a history of your credit: Equifax, Experian, and TransUnion. You can obtain your report from each of these companies individually or you can obtain the reports from all three companies at once. Each agency accumulates the information in a slightly different way. This service is free and is provided once a year. The phone number is 877-322-8228. (Go to www.PurpleRibbonPublishing.com for more information.) When you receive the reports, study them thoroughly. If you find an error, address it immediately. An example of an error is your phone company indicates you have been late with payments. You know this to be untrue. Locate evidence to prove otherwise, make copies, and send the information to the individual credit bureaus and they will contact the phone company. If there is a credit card listed that you did not open, contact the reporting agency and they will contact the company who issued the card. It is then up to the company to prove you opened the credit card. This can be a frustrating process, but it is important to address and finalize.

Credit score:

A credit score is calculated using all factors detailed in the credit report. Each of the three credit reporting agencies will calculate your credit score. This score measures your ability to repay debt and determines whether or not you are a risk to a lender. Credit scores range from 300-850, with the lower number indicating more risk and the higher number indicating less risk. Here is an example of the ranking:

**Credit Score Ranking:**
800 or above -Exceptional
740-799- Very good
670-739 -Acceptable
580-669 - Fair
Less than 580 - Poor

What impact does your credit report and credit score have?
Your credit score signals to lenders your ability to repay debt. It is an indicator of the actions that you will likely take with your money.

A creditor, which is a financial institution such as a bank or credit card company, will use this information to determine whether you are a consumer who will pay back debt in a timely manner. If your report shows missed payments, then companies will view you as a riskier customer, and they may lend to you at a much higher interest rate. The company needs to be compensated for the additional risk they perceive based on your credit history. This will affect you going forward because it compounds your financial problem.

If you have a strong credit report and score (very good and exceptional ranking), you will have more financial freedom and will be able to access money by borrowing either through loans or credit cards. You will also be paying a lower interest rate, which makes it cheaper for you to borrow, leading to lower monthly bills.

For example, if you have an 'excellent' credit score, a current interest rate on a new car loan would be around 3%. If you are borrowing $25,000 for 60 months, your monthly car payment would be $427.

If you have a 'poor' credit score, a current interest rate on a new car loan would be around 7%. If you are borrowing $25,000 for 60 months, your monthly car payment would be $495. Over the 5 year period, this adds up to $4,080 in additional interest.

If you have a low credit score due to a partner mishandling your finances, you can present documentation to a creditor illustrating your current ability to repay, such as an employment contract and current expenses. This may help you obtain a loan, and one with a lower rate, even without a strong credit history.

## What about credit card payments?

Look at the following table. The interest rate paid (APR) varies according to the credit score. This example shows the length of time until payoff and the amount of interest people with different credit scores pay for a $5,000 credit card balance, paying the minimum amount due. I applied 5% as the minimum amount due for this example. 5% of $5,000 is a $250 minimum monthly payment.

The exceptional credit score scenario is paying $1,898 in interest over the time frame. The poor credit scenario is paying $3,447 in interest which is almost double. The difference in interest paid between an exceptional credit score and a poor credit score is $1,549.

| Credit Score Ranking | Credit Card Rate | Balance Payoff | Total Payment |
|---|---|---|---|
| Exceptional | 16.90% | 100 months | $6,898 |
| Poor | 24.90% | 121 months | $8,447 |

How can you strengthen your credit score?

It will take time and patience to increase your score. Pay off accounts with low balances. Do not apply for another credit card. Too many credit cards can hurt your score. It is also advantageous to set up automatic payments of recurring bills to ensure they are paid on time. Don't just move your debt around, but try to set up a plan to pay it off. Consolidate by transferring balances to one credit card, the one with the lowest interest rate.

What if you don't have a credit score?

No credit score means you have no credit history. You haven't taken out any loans in your name. While this isn't a bad thing and many young people fall into this category, there is no history of timely payments. The easiest way to build a credit score is to obtain a credit card from your bank, use it consistently, and pay it off in full on time. Doing this will establish a high credit score.

Why do we have debt?

There are many good reasons to borrow money. Instead of saving for a long period of time toward a goal, people can borrow a lump sum and pay it off monthly. Borrowing money for a home is often essential. Most prospective homeowners can afford monthly mortgage payments, but can't save for the entire cost of a home. Saving the total price for a car can also be difficult and often unattainable. Often the cost of large purchase items will be borrowed.

Money for big ticket items, often seen as needs, can be borrowed. It is not advisable however, to borrow money for things considered 'wants' such as a vacation, new clothes, or even restaurant visits. These expenses add up quickly and you may find yourself in much deeper debt than you realized.

### Tips for using credit cards:

Pay off in full each month. Take advantage of what credit card companies have to offer. Choose a credit card with a rewards program that suits you. For example, if you travel often, rewards such as frequent flyer miles would benefit you. Many cash back rewards credit cards are available. Some credit cards give bonus cash back when you consistently pay your bill on time. The Target card offers an immediate 5% discount on Target purchases. Many other cards offer cash back programs, such as Discover card. Shop around for credit deals.

Be sure to choose a 'no annual fee' credit card, unless you are certain you will receive more in discounts than the annual fee. There are some airline credit cards that offer a certain number of free miles upon opening the credit card. Sometimes these bonuses can be worth more than the annual cost. Read through the descriptions and the 'fine print'. There are several websites that rate credit card offers. If credit card debt could become a problem for you, it is a better option to have no credit cards for emergencies and rely solely on cash.

### Tackling the debt:

In a previous exercise, you totaled your loan and credit card balances. You also created a list of assets. After gathering these, we analyzed your financial situation. If you missed any additional debt that you were not aware of, it would have shown up when running your credit report. You can add that data now. Analyze your debt again. Let's focus on credit card debt. Once the credit cards are paid off, you can focus on other debt. Look at the interest rates on your debt and start paying off the highest interest debt. Are you paying a high interest rate for a car loan? If so, start to work on paying the loan down.

List your debts in order from the highest interest rate (APR) to the lowest. Look at the minimum monthly payments. Notice the total outstanding balances due for each account.

Ways to pay down your high interest debt:
- In Chapter 5, you created a list of your total assets and calculated your account balances. Can you use money from your savings or checking account to pay off the credit card debt? Savings accounts yield almost no return while the credit cards have high interest rates and penalties. Why have savings (no matter the amount) sitting in an account when it could be actively reducing compounding interest? What about a Certificate of Deposit (CD)? If you have one coming due soon, use that money to pay off the high interest debt. If you hold an investment account not related to your retirement, use that money to pay down the credit card debt. You may have to pay taxes on any capital gains you've earned on your investment.

- Call and talk with a representative at your credit card company to set up a payment plan that offers a lower interest rate. Work with each credit card company to secure a lower rate. These companies have incentives to work with you. They would rather get paid than have you default.

- Consolidate all of your credit card debt to a lower interest rate loan. If your credit score is good, secure a personal loan from a bank or credit union to pay all debt, allowing you to then work on repaying one and one only. Having one loan simplifies your debt situation significantly.

- Contact a nonprofit counseling service such as the National Foundation for Credit Counseling (www.NFCC.org) 800-388-2227, or Consumer Credit Counseling Services (www.Credit.org/CCCS/) 800-431-8157. They can assist with obtaining a debt management plan. More information is available at www.PurpleRibbonPublishing.com.

- In Chapters 6 and 7, you identified ways to increase your total income and decrease your total expenses. What was the net income? Remember, your net income is calculated by subtracting expenses from income. The remainder of income after expenses are paid each month should be used to pay down the credit card with the highest interest rate.

- Remember the extra paychecks that were pointed out in Chapter 3? If you are paid weekly or bi-weekly, you have extra checks that were not included in your monthly income. When you receive an extra paycheck, pay off some of your debt.

- You could obtain a home equity line of credit to pay off your credit cards. A home equity line of credit is a great way to pay off debt because the interest rate will be lower and the interest payments are tax-deductible for those who itemize taxes. You are able to borrow a certain percentage of the total equity in your home, usually around 80%. One big disadvantage is that the equity is a buffer and gives you much more financial stability. However, if you are serious about paying off your high interest debt, this is certainly a viable option.

- When you examined your expenses and looked at your home situation, did you consider selling your home and either going into a less expensive home or apartment? If so, does the sale yield additional money? You could use that cash to pay off high interest debt.

- Are you contributing to a 529 Plan for your child's education? You need to take care of yourself first. Pay down high interest debt before saving for college unless your divorce decree requires you to do so.

- I caution you when considering this next idea. If you have been contributing to your retirement account, consider rerouting those additional payments to pay off high interest loans. Make sure you are not falling into the trap of spending more because of 'perceived' additional income. As soon as the high interest debt is paid off, return to investing in your retirement.

- Bankruptcy. There are two types of bankruptcy: Chapter 7 and Chapter 13. Filing for bankruptcy is a huge decision and the consequences last for a long time. Filing for bankruptcy does not automatically erase all debt. Some debts are not dischargeable. The bankruptcy is public domain and will stay on your credit report for ten years when filing Chapter 7. If you file for Chapter 13 bankruptcy it will remain on your credit report for seven years. This process will avert attempts to obtain any type of loan, and, your credit score will fall. Bankruptcy should ONLY be used if all other options fail. Seek professional advice if considering this path. Not all debts are forgiven in certain types of bankruptcy. More information is available at PurpleRibbonPublishing.com.

- We have only briefly gone over taxes and haven't addressed your tax return. Ideally, you should only receive a small dollar amount, because you want to pay the taxes required throughout the year, rather than a bulk amount at the end of the year. Consult with a tax accountant if you are not sure how many exemptions to claim. There are free services for low- income taxpayers.

Your refund should immediately be utilized to reduce other debt. This is money that you have not budgeted in your income, so use it wisely. Many use the refund to purchase new furniture or put a down payment on a car. This is not a wise move when credit card debt exists.

During this process, cease using the high interest credit cards. Do not use any credit cards while paying off debt. Switch to a debit card or even better use cash.

Once your credit card debt is paid off, look at any other debt you may have. Do you have a personal loan or student loans that you feel should be paid off? Go through the strategies that you just completed and pay off this debt, too.

You have just absorbed a great deal of information pertaining to your debt. Counseling services are available if you feel overwhelmed. The more you understand and are aware of your finances, the better equipped you will be to efficiently and effectively repair your problems.

$ Obtain credit report and take care of any errors
$ Find out your credit score
$ Review strategies to pay down debt

## Emotional Health

Dealing with debt can be very stressful and overwhelming. A reduction of the debt will ease a measure of that stress. It will be rewarding when you see balances decreasing. With diligence and discipline you will get there.

Downtime and personal time are so important. Be sure to take part in relaxing activities. Read, work on crafts, watch movies, join social media, reach out to friends with whom you have lost contact, or spend time with friends and family. You could start a project you've always wanted to try. You don't have to spend money. It is a great time to do something for you.

Becoming financially independent and enjoying stress-relieving experiences will improve your overall health and quality of life.

**EXERCISE:** Identify 3 free activities that can reduce your stress. They may be emotional experiences such as getting together with friends and talking, or taking a bubble bath with lighted candles surrounding you.

# Chapter 9
## *Savings And Goals*

In this section, you will focus on your upcoming needs and wants. Look beyond today. What do you hope your life will be like in 5 years, 10 years, 25 years? Your goals will be different from others. Goals are fluid. As you age and your situation changes, so will your goals.

Listed below are examples of goals:

Purchase a new car
Family vacation
College tuition
Renovate kitchen
Holiday gifts
Pay off debt
Save for retirement

In Chapter 5, we looked at your assets and liabilities. If you currently have high interest debt, your first step is to work diligently to reduce the debt by applying the ideas offered in the previous chapter.

Maybe you already have a substantial amount of savings. If so, discover the advantages of allocating savings between low risk-low interest accounts and higher risk-higher return accounts to make your money work for you.

### Saving For Emergencies

Unfortunately, things happen. Preparation is key. To avoid the necessary step of debt in these instances, build up a savings account that is only used for certain expenses and emergencies.

Experts say you should have the equivalent of at least three months (many say six to nine) of expenses saved in an account that can be accessed without penalty. So, if your expenses are $2,000 per month, you should have at least $6,000 emergency money in an account.

Why? If something happens to your health, your job, or you incur a major bill, such as legal fees, car repairs, or home issues, you will have the money to pay the bill instead of going into debt and incurring interest expenses.

Saving three months of expenses in advance is difficult for most people to achieve, but it is something to work toward as you make progress with your financial plan.

Start with an easier goal. Can you put a certain amount of money aside each week to start the savings account? Maybe $10?

Once you have saved an emergency buffer, let's think about other reasons you need to save.

## Saving For Children's College Education

Does your divorce decree stipulate you are required to save for a portion of your child's/children's college tuition? Is saving for this a priority to you? Let me caution you. It is wise to address your own financial situation before your child's. I am a mother and I understand the desire to give your children everything you possibly can. However, if I am not taking care of my current financial situation first, then it is irresponsible of me to spend money elsewhere. We need to look at the total financial picture and see where we stand. Look back at your assets. How well-funded is your retirement account? Are you financially stable right now? Do you have an emergency account?

In the absence of saved college tuition, where all your efforts were otherwise focused on creating a debt-free life, your child will have the opportunity to apply for a student loan. The interest rate is generally low, and by the time your child graduates, your financial situation will be so improved, you will be in a position to assist with the payments of the student loan.

If you are determined to save for their college, consider a college savings plan, such as a 529 plan. There are tax advantages to setting up this type of account. The money can be used for almost any type of college, including community colleges. Also, the funds can be transferred to one of your other children if needed. For more information, go to www.PurpleRibbonPublishing.com and follow links to websites with more information.

## Home Purchase

Depending on the housing situation you are in after divorce, you might be considering purchasing a home. You will need to save for a down payment and the initial costs of moving into a home, such as moving expenses, furniture and closing costs. One advantage to home ownership is that the interest paid on the mortgage, the property taxes, and the school taxes are all tax deductible. This essentially lowers the cost of owning a home.

## New Car

Do you need a new car? Generally you can purchase a new car with no down payment, unless your credit history is weak. However, you might want to put a down payment on the purchase to lower the monthly payments and interest rate. You will need to set aside that money.

If you are thinking about purchasing a car, have you decided on new or used? There are advantages and disadvantages to each. A new car generally comes with a warranty, is more reliable, offers a lower interest rate, and can normally be purchased without a down payment. A big disadvantage is that automobiles depreciate in value very quickly.

Often a used car only a couple of years old can be purchased for about half of the price of a new car. You could purchase a used 2013 Toyota Camry for about half the price of a 2016 Toyota Camry.

## Vacation

Are you planning a vacation? It is unwise to borrow money to pay for 'wants' such as a vacation. As much as you would like to take a vacation, you should only do so if it doesn't put you in debt or take away from your emergency savings. Make sure to allocate money for a vacation if this is a priority for you.

## Taxes and Extra Paychecks

Remember the tax refunds and extra paychecks some women receive? If you are paid weekly or bi-weekly, then you should have two to four extra paychecks each year because your monthly bills are paid with wages from four weeks of pay. Are you receiving funds from another job? Has the difference between your income and expenses widened? If you do not have debt, use all of those proceeds to save money. You can fund your emergency savings account and then start saving for your other goals.

## Retirement

Are you saving for retirement? Saving is essential. There are websites that illustrate how much money you need to have saved for retirement based on your current living expenses. Over time, your investments will grow and compound. Starting earlier ensures you need only to invest smaller amounts throughout the years. Starting late requires larger investment sums.

Let me give you an example. Suppose you are twenty-five years old, you start to save $3,000 each year for retirement, and are able to earn an average of 8% per year for forty years. At age sixty-five, you will have approximately $777,000 in your retirement account.

Now suppose you don't start saving for retirement until you are thirty-five years old. You save $3,000 each year, earning 8% interest for thirty years. At age sixty-five your account will be valued at about $340,000. This is a $437,000 difference! From age 25 to 35, you deposited $3,000 per year, or a total of $30,000. That $30,000 would have grown into an additional $437,000. This illustrates the time value of money. The earlier you invest, the longer your money has time to grow.

If you are older and haven't yet started to save for retirement, there is still time to catch up. Certain retirement plans have 'catch-up' clauses and allow you to invest more money than younger people. Saving money is difficult, especially if you are on a tight budget. But it is not impossible, and is very important for your financial future.

There is favorable tax treatment when you're saving with a qualified retirement account which differs from saving money in a bank. Certain types of retirement accounts take pre-tax earnings and place them into the account that grows tax-deferred. This means that you do not pay taxes on the earnings of the investment while it grows.

There are four main types of retirement plans available to you. Your employer, especially if it is a small company, might have a different retirement account than those listed. Please talk to your human resources department to obtain details.

They are as follows:
- 401k
- 403b
- Traditional IRA (Investment Retirement Account)
- Roth IRA

### 401k and 403b Retirement Accounts

Both 401k's and 403b's are company sponsored plans. The difference between the two is that 401k's are offered by for-profit companies and 403b's are offered for employees of educational institutions and some tax-exempt organizations.

The key to these plans is that your contributions are invested pre-tax and the investments grow tax deferred. This means that your money grows more quickly.

For both of these plans, you can invest up to $18,000 (as of 2016) and if you are over fifty years of age, you can contribute an additional $6,000 to 'catch up.'

### Traditional IRAs (Individual Retirement Accounts)

Another type of retirement account is called a Traditional IRA. This type of account can be opened at a bank or brokerage firm. Depending on your income, the contribution can be tax deductible. The maximum contribution is $5,500 per year or $6,500 per year if you are fifty years or older. You can start to make withdrawals at age fifty-nine-and-a-half and are required to make withdrawals by age seventy-and-a-half. You cannot make contributions after that age. You will pay taxes on the withdrawals.

### Roth IRAs

Roth IRAs can also be opened at banks and brokerage firms and the contribution limits are the same. The maximum contribution for both IRAs combined is $5,500 per year or $6,500 per year if you are fifty years or older. You can invest $2,000 in a Traditional IRA and $3,500 in a Roth IRA if you are under age fifty.

Roth IRAs differ from Traditional IRAs regarding their tax implications. Roth IRAs are funded with after-tax earnings. The money grows tax free and when you withdraw you do not pay federal taxes. The maximum contribution is the same as the Traditional IRA. However, you can make contributions forever and are not required to withdraw the money.

There is more flexibility in withdrawing money from a Roth IRA than with the Traditional IRA. Meeting certain requirements means you can withdraw money that has been invested for five years. Consult with a professional when withdrawing money early to make sure it qualifies as penalty-free and not subject to taxes. Some examples of this type of withdrawal are: pay for a first-time home purchase, pay for qualified medical expenses and educational expenses, or if you become disabled. There is a maximum allowable withdrawal amount.

Evaluate your situation to identify which account suits your savings needs best.

What types of investments do you purchase via your retirement account?

Now that you've opened up and funded your retirement account, either through you employer or at a bank or brokerage firm, you need to decide how to invest the funds. There are many options available. They range from very conservative to very risky. You will see your account fluctuate as the investments change value. Depending on your age and risk aversion, you will want to invest accordingly. Seek advice from a financial representative when you open the account, but here is an overview of investments from the lowest risk to the highest.

**Lowest Risk**—The lowest risk investments are cash equivalents, such as savings accounts, money market accounts, Treasury bills, and certificates of deposit (CDs). These are safe investments, but provide a very low return.

**Medium Risk**—Bonds are considered riskier than cash equivalents because bonds are the debt of a company or government and sometimes, but rarely, are not repaid. Bonds earn a higher yield than cash equivalents.

**Highest Risk**—Stocks make up the riskiest segment of investing. Stocks are traded securities whose value is dependent on the profits of the underlying company. The state of the economy also affects stock prices. Historically, a diversified portfolio of stocks has had higher returns than the lower risk investments. However, the volatility of stocks is much higher than other investments, and therefore the investor is being compensated for the risk by receiving higher returns over a period of time.

It is recommended that you choose a combination of all three, based on your risk preference and age.

The best way to purchase these investments is to invest in mutual funds. Essentially mutual funds are a large group of investments that you own a small portion of. For example, you might purchase a stock mutual fund which would be made up of the stocks of many companies. You would own a tiny portion of each company. The big advantage to mutual funds is that they are diversified. Diversification is spreading risk over several assets. If one stock goes down considerably you still have many others to offset that decrease.

Over time, you will want to adjust your asset allocations by moving your investments into the lower risk classes. See the table that follows. Notice in this example at age 20, the account has 80% in stocks, 15% in bonds, and 5% in cash, and as the person ages, the percentage invested in stocks decreases. This is dependent on your personal assessment of risk. If you prefer less risk, you would have a higher amount of your investment in cash equivalents and bonds. As you age, you move the investments into more conservative assets in order to protect the growth of your investment.

## Asset Allocation Table

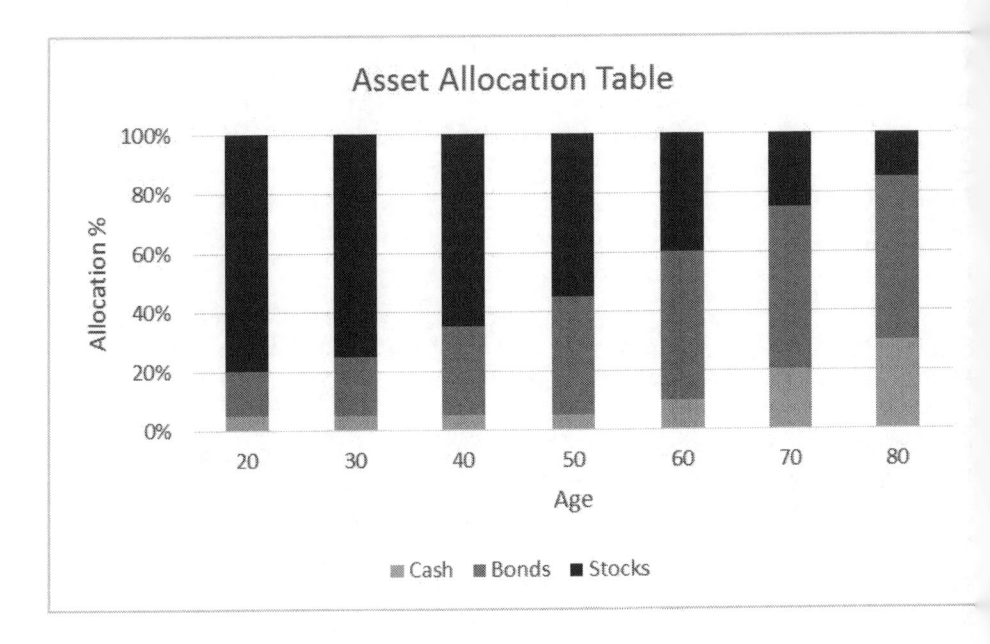

*Bar chart showing allocation percentages (Cash, Bonds, Stocks) by Age (20, 30, 40, 50, 60, 70, 80).*

## Long Term Planning

Wills, guardians and beneficiaries were touched on in Chapter 1. Now you will learn more detailed specifics of estate planning. This is an unpleasant subject to think about, but once you have made your arrangements, you will feel much better. This is especially true for women with children under the age of eighteen.

It is essential that you make a Last Will and Testament. If you do not have one, and you pass away, the state will determine the division of your assets.

Depending on your level of assets, the age of your children and other factors, you may decide to put your assets in a trust.

A power of attorney—financial and healthcare—is also essential to have in case you become incapacitated. A close relative, an adult child, or a trusted friend would be an appropriate person to ask.

## Life Insurance

When you purchase life insurance you are paying premiums and in exchange when you die, the company will pay out a death benefit to your beneficiaries. If you have dependents, you absolutely need life insurance. In Chapter 1, the need to designate a guardian to care for your children was discussed. Life insurance helps prevent financial burden for the guardian.

## How Much Do You Need To Purchase?

Ideally, the appropriate amount will cover your children's needs based on their ages. Consider expenses up to the age of eighteen, and possibly their college expenses. Their guardian will incur extra expenses of maintaining a home big enough for your children. Activities, food and clothing will cost money. This financial burden can be lessened with the right amount of insurance. Without dependents, the amount of life insurance you will need to purchase changes. Do you want to leave your grown children money? What about money for grandchildren? This is a personal decision.

Talk to an insurance agent about how much coverage you need. One way to figure out an estimate is to multiply your earnings by ten and then adjust upward if you have more than one or two children and if you have a lot of debt. How much do you have in investments and real estate right now? Assets allow for the consideration of a smaller, less expensive policy.

First, check with your employer to see if you have a life insurance benefit. Some companies include one in their benefits package.

## Different Types Of Life Insurance

There are two main types of life insurance: term life policy and permanent life policy.

### Term Life Policy

If you die within a specific period of time, your beneficiaries get paid the death benefit that you purchased. For example, if you are 40 and you purchase a 20 year policy worth $200,000, you will pay a set amount each year for 20 years. If you die before age 60, your beneficiaries will get the $200,000. If you die after age 60, there is no payout.

Term life insurance is inexpensive and easy to purchase. The younger and healthier you are, the less expensive it is.

The main disadvantage of this type of insurance is that after the term expires, you no longer have insurance and have to renew (at a higher cost) if you want to retain the insurance. The best strategy is to anticipate how long you want coverage to last when first buying it.

## Permanent Life Policy

When you purchase a permanent life policy, and there are several types including whole life and universal life, you are purchasing an insurance policy that will cover you for the term of you natural life. As long as you pay your premiums, your beneficiaries will receive the death benefit regardless of your age at death.

There are several advantages to this type of policy. It is a savings vehicle. You can borrow against the cash value or withdraw the cash value based on the investment earnings and the account growth. There are many options, and depending on the type of permanent insurance purchased, they will differ.

The main disadvantage is that it is very costly and if used as a savings vehicle, you will receive lower returns than other investments would yield. Purchasing life insurance requires you to really think about your beneficiaries' needs and your wishes.

We've studied the details of savings, retirement accounts, and investing the money. These can be difficult and confusing topics. Estate planning is also a very powerful topic because you are taking control. Each step we've taken in this book is leading you closer to financial freedom.

- $ Are you starting to save for emergencies?
- $ Investing in your retirement?
- $ Purchasing life insurance?

## Emotional Health

It can be frustrating thinking about saving money while struggling to balance your budget and/or pay down your credit cards. This increases our stress level and stress can impact our bodies in many negative ways. How have you dealt with the stress? Have you identified positive coping mechanisms?

**EXERCISE:** Think about the future when your financial situation will be greatly improved. Dare yourself to dream. What would you like to save for? What are your future goals?

List 3 things you would like to save for.

# Part 5

*Putting It All Together*

# Chapter 10
## *Wrapping Up*

Each step taken in this book has provided you with detailed information about your finances. When informed, you can more accurately decide on the next step. Now that you know where you stand, both with your current finances and your long-term goals, you can make educated and less emotional decisions.

A financial plan reduces stress. Think about how overwhelmed you felt at the beginning of the book. Knowledge really is power. You have the power to make good choices that will yield great results.

It takes sacrifice to be financially free, but the reward is worth it. Your stress levels will decrease and you will gain confidence and peace of mind.
As your needs and situation change, reevaluate. This is a fluid process. As your finances become more stable, you can change your goals. You will be financially free in no time!

Final Tips: Remember to make sure everything is in your name, and your name alone. Double check and run your credit report every year. Be safe! Stay organized. Keep working on increasing your income and reducing spending. Let the difference between your income and spending expand. If you need help with debt, please seek it. Remember to start an emergency savings account and let it grow. Retirement is very important. Little sacrifices today will yield big dividends in the future.

## Emotional Health

Congratulations! You have completed the book and learned so much about taking care of yourself financially. Do not expect to have grasped all—or even most—of the concepts I have included when working through the steps. It may require a second read-through for you to fully understand all processes, motivations and disciplines, and results. It is important to take care of your financial, emotional, and physical health.

**EXERCISE:** Celebrate your success!

# APPENDIX A

I'd like to address an all too common occurrence: domestic violence also referred to as domestic abuse or intimate partner violence. Both women and men can be victims of domestic violence, but I will focus on women as the victims in this section. There are several types of abuse and all are damaging. If you have left an abuser, please take appropriate steps to ensure your safety and privacy.

Change your passwords on all accounts, including email, social media and bank accounts. Disable your phone GPS and do not post your location on social media. If you have an Order of Protection, keep it with you at all times and call the police if it is breached. If you have shared custody, arrange pick up and drop off of the children at a safe public place, such as a police station.

*Freeing Yourself Financially* is about taking control of your personal finances. Sometimes in a relationship one partner controls all of the finances. If your partner has excluded you from your personal finances, you might have been experiencing **financial abuse**.

Abuse is all about control, power and manipulation. What better way to gain power than by cutting off access to family finances?

Listed below are just some examples of financial abuse:

Preventing the victim from working.
Forcing the victim to give the abuser her paycheck.
Making her account for all spending and putting the victim on a strict budget.
Giving the victim a small allowance.
Denying the victim access to information on family finances. The abuser controls all money and financial decisions. The abuser runs up credit card bills.
The abuser ruins the victim's credit.

All of these examples show the victim losing control of an important part of her livelihood. If she isn't allowed to work, her social contact is limited and she cannot advance in her profession. She becomes more dependent on her partner financially.

When the abuser controls the amount of money spent, the victim is placed into a difficult position. It takes away her choices and freedom. Also, if she spends more money than 'allocated,' she risks abuse.

Having no control over the family budget implies she is beneath the abuser and is just a possession.

Ruining the victim's credit cripples the victim and can prevent her from leaving the abuser because of financial reasons. This fulfills the abuser's motive of gaining power and control in the relationship.
Have you been in this situation?
You are now learning how to be in control of your finances.
You set the rules now.

There are other types of abuse.

**Physical violence** is not only hitting or punching. Many actions fall under the umbrella of physical violence, such as: pushing, throwing things at the victim, pulling hair, grabbing and squeezing the body, choking, kicking, physically preventing the victim from leaving.

How common is physical violence? The statistics are shocking. '1 in 4 women (24.3%) and 1 in 7 men (13.8%) aged 18 and older in the United States have been the victim of severe physical violence by an intimate partner in their lifetime.' (1) This is unacceptable.

**Sexual abuse** is any unwanted sexual act. It includes and is not limited to rape, coercion of the victim to commit sexual acts, the abuser making sexual threats, and not allowing the victim the use of contraception. These are only a few examples.

The numbers are surprisingly high for sexual abuse. Nearly one in 10 women has been raped by an intimate partner in her lifetime, including completed forced penetration, attempted forced penetration or alcohol/drug-facilitated completed penetration. (2)

**Emotional and mental abuse** are thought to be on a spectrum that stretches from very mild to extreme. This type of abuse is very damaging to the psyche and often is said to have longer term damage than physical abuse. Usually emotional abuse continues to get worse because the abuser attains their goal of control and power.

This abuse covers many areas with the end result leading to the victim feeling belittled and void of self-esteem. The abuser works to control the victim through blaming, withholding, judging, being extremely jealous, and denying conversations ever took place, just to name a few examples.

**Verbal abuse** is characterized by an abuser's explosive nature toward the victim. The victim often does not understand what sets off the abuser. Yelling, put downs and arguing until the abuser 'wins' or the victim gives in are some examples. Uncontrolled anger and threats are also characteristics of verbal abuse.

**Psychological abuse** is often called 'gaslighting.' Gaslighting happens when the abuser repeatedly denies the truth and makes a concerted effort to have the victim doubt their observations and instincts. This makes victims doubt themselves which leads to uncertainty in all elements of their lives. Examples are: "When did I say that?" "You must be making that up." "That never happened." "What are you talking about? It didn't happen that way." "You're doing this on purpose. You're trying to start an argument."

There are several forms of gaslighting. They include:

• Withholding—the abuser decides not to listen or doesn't discuss his/her feelings.
• Countering—the abuser tells the victim that their memory is warped and the event didn't happen like that.
• Blocking/Diverting—the abuser changes the conversation and controls the conversation.
• Trivializing—the abuser makes the victim feel their opinions and needs aren't important.
• Forgetting/Denial—the abuser conveniently forgets conversations or promises made.

Most of the time the victim doesn't recognize what is happening, but they can feel that something isn't right. As gaslighting continues the victim begins to second guess everything they say, do, and believe and their self-esteem slowly crumbles. They wonder if they are too sensitive and start apologizing for things they think or say. This is exactly what the abuser wants to happen. It is a form of control and manipulation, though subtle and gradual. The victim becomes more vulnerable and insecure and is more likely to stay in the relationship.

**Spiritual abuse** is seen when an abuser uses religion to keep the victim in the relationship and controlled. Feeling 'guilted' to stay in a marriage because of the marital vows is a common example of spiritual abuse. The abuser distorts Biblical Scripture to try to prove that the relationship should be continued, when it's apparent that it should not.

**Stalking** is repeated, unwanted attention. The stalker can either be a former intimate partner, an acquaintance, or a stranger. He or she repeatedly pursues the victim through many different means.

Stalking can include:
- following,
- showing up at home or work uninvited,
- sending texts, emails, or calling when the abuser has been told to stop,
- sending unwanted presents,
- tracking by some form of GPS or locating device,
- damaging belongings,
- threatening safety,
- threatening to kidnap the children.

Stalking and domestic violence. 81% of women stalked by a current or former intimate partner are also physically assaulted by that partner. (3) Stalkers can make their behavior look justified. They know the patterns and behaviors of the victim. Also, when children are involved, the stalker has more access to their victim and stalking can intensify.

What should you do if you're being stalked?

Write everything down in a log book. Keep track of all contact with the stalk- er. Save text messages, emails, voice mails, unwanted presents, and anything else that can be used as evidence. Change patterns and consider staying in someone else's home where you can't be located. Contact the authorities and provide your log book. Stalking is a crime and must be taken seriously.

If you have experienced any form of domestic violence, please seek help. Often domestic violence organizations offer free confidential counseling. Reach out to someone. Domestic violence is very damaging to your self-confidence, and can create great difficulty when attempting to form and hold healthy relationships in the future.

1) http://www.cdc.gov/violenceprevention/intimatepartnerviolence/consequences.html

2) Tjaden, Patricia & Thoennes, Nancy. National Institute of Justice and the Centers of Disease Control and Prevention, "Extent, Nature and Consequences Of Intimate Partner Violence: Findings From the National Violence Against Women Survey." (2000)

3) Tjaden, Patricia & Thoennes, Nancy. (1998). "Stalking in America." National Institute For Justice.

## APPENDIX B
# Examples of expenses

Housing:
Home mortgage (including taxes and insurance), Home equity line of credit loan, HOA fees, Rent, Renters insurance

Utilities:
Electric/Gas, Water/Sewer, Phone, Internet, Cable

Home maintenance:
Landscaping/Snow removal, Home cleaning supplies/cleaner, Household items/furniture

Transportation:
Car loan(s), Car insurance, Gas for car, Oil changes, Repairs, Parking, Tolls, Public transportation

Groceries and Restaurants

Personal items:
Clothes, Shoes, Suits, Jackets, Purses, Briefcases, Other accessories
Personal care products (ex: Shampoo, deodorant), Haircuts, Mani/Pedi

Medical:
Copays, Prescriptions, Dentist, Eye doctor, Glasses/Contacts

Children:
Child care, After-school care, Activities, Lessons, Tutoring, Sports equipment, Music accessories

Gifts

Education:
Prepaid college savings, any college tuition or classes, Workshops, Seminars

Family fun:
Movies, Fitness club membership, Hobbies, Museums, Theme parks, Bowling, Mag subscriptions, Books, DVD rentals

Vacation

Pets:
Food, Vet, Other types of animals--horses, etc

Donations

Lawyer

For more information about the author and the supplemental articles and information, please go to www.PurpleRibbonPublishing.com.

## Acknowledgments

Many people have helped *Freeing Yourself Financially* come to fruition. I'd like to thank my husband, Rodney, and two sons, Branden and Justin for their continued support and love. My mother read and edited *Freeing Yourself Financially* several times and she deserves special recognition.

Family members and friends have helped with the editing process as well. Thank you to Donna, Faith, Heather, Sandra, Sarah, and Susan. Sheila Kennedy was instrumental in getting *Freeing Yourself Financially* off the ground and helping to raise awareness to this financial guide.

A special thank you to PT Editing.

I could not have done it without **all** of your help.

Thank you!

Made in the USA
Middletown, DE
02 June 2017